This Happy S

This book is dedicated to the memory of
David Powell
1925 - 2012
whose quiet work helped to ensure Clare's place
among the major poets

THIS HAPPY SPIRIT

POEMS BY JOHN CLARE

Selected and Edited by

R. K. R. Thornton

and

Carry Akroyd

illustrated by

Carry Akroyd

2013

THE JOHN CLARE SOCIETY

This Happy Spirit 2013

ISBN 978-0-9564113-3-4

©2013 Introduction & selection R. K. R Thornton

©2013 Illustrations Carry Akroyd

The John Clare Society
Helpston, Peterborough
www.johnclare.org.uk

Printed by Lightning Source

Set in Calisto MT

CONTENTS

INTRODUCTION

It is still a matter of amazement that John Clare, who started with so many disadvantages, should have become one of the major poets of the nineteenth century, to be placed alongside Wordsworth, Keats, and the other great Romantics.

He was born in Northamptonshire in the village of Helpston (boundary changes now put it in Cambridgeshire), the son of a totally illiterate mother and a peasant father, a thresher, who could read the Bible but little else, though he knew many folk songs. The family lived in a quarter of a cottage and was grindingly poor, so that they could not pay for much education for their son, though they sent him to school when they could. His schooling, perhaps for three months of each year, might seem inadequate, but something about his eagerness to read and the lessons that he received set him on the road to a delight in poetry. It was at the school in nearby Glinton that he first met Mary Joyce, the woman who was to become the ideal love of his life and his muse, though he was not allowed to court her and she died unmarried many years later. At the age of about thirteen (dates are difficult to be accurate about in his early life) he discovered that a weaver in the village had a copy of James Thomson's poem *The Seasons,* and Clare later wrote that reading the opening of 'Spring' made his heart 'twitter with joy'. He began to write his own poems, sometimes on the paper bags in which his mother bought sugar. He saved up his small resources to buy writing paper rather than sweetmeats and fruit, but he could not always afford the three farthings for decent paper. He read his poems to his parents without telling them they were his, so that he might

1

get from them an unbiased idea of whether they were intelligible and worth keeping.

He did indeed keep them, eventually in a large blank book that he bought from a local bookseller, who began to be curious about his writing. In due course the poems came to the notice of another Stamford bookseller and through him to the London publisher John Taylor, who had already brought out the work of John Keats. Clare's poems were published in 1820 and were an immediate success, going into four editions and selling 3000 copies while Keats's latest volume sold only 500.

Despite the sudden success and national fame, Clare's troubles were not over. He married Patty Turner soon after the publication of his first book in 1820, and his family grew quickly. Although he received an annual payment from the local aristocracy, and a fund was set up to provide him with an annuity, money was never easy and the pressures of fame, work, writing, providing for his family, and public curiosity disturbed him. His second book, rushed out on the success of the first, sold less well, and his third book, *The Shepherd's Calendar* (1827), took years of stressful revision and argument, but sold even more poorly. By the time of his fourth book *The Rural Muse* (1835) his popularity had faded, his publisher had turned to other things, and he was ill. His friends began to worry about his mental health and placed him in Matthew Allen's asylum in Essex. After four years he left Allen's establishment and in four days, with poor shoes, little food and no comfortable place to sleep, he walked nearly a hundred miles back to his home in Northborough. But being at home did not work out and he was committed to Northampton General Lunatic Asylum in 1844, which he never subsequently left until his death in 1864. While in the asylum, he continued to write.

This rapid sketch of his life glosses over crucial details. His writing was the way in which he understood the world about him; it was a necessary part of his existence. When the doctor filled in the admission papers for Northampton and read the question: 'Was it [his illness] preceded by any severe or long-continued mental emotion or exertion?' he noted: 'after years addicted to Poetical prosing'. The crucial word here is 'addicted'. Clare could not exist without writing.

Second, it does not hint at the sheer volume of his writing. The Oxford English Texts edition of Clare's poems, which Eric Robinson, David Powell and others completed after nearly forty years' work, runs to nine volumes, over 3,000 poems. The majority of them were never printed in his lifetime, and when his poetry was published, the text was usually 'corrected', with the danger of losing Clare's essential character. Another aspect of the mass of poems is a certain amount of repetitiveness, and a slight roughness, not surprising when one remembers that these are working documents amassed over many years.

Last, we need to emphasize his subject matter. He wrote about the world as he knew it in and around Helpston, the countryside, with its birds, animals, flowers, trees and those who lived and worked there, and the impact on them of political decisions way beyond the ordinary man's control. He was always conscious of the rapid changes that were taking place, particularly the enclosure of the fields, which changed both the physical and political lie of the land. He writes as if he is the spokesman of the land itself. Amid all the pains and problems of his life, he retained a wonderful capacity to take joy in what he saw and to reflect that joy in his poetry. As he describes himself in 'The Peasant Poet' with which *The Wood is Sweet* ends:

> A silent man in life's affairs,
>   A thinker from a boy,
> A peasant in his daily cares –
>   The poet in his joy.

It is this aspect which we have aimed to represent in our new selection from his poetry, to make a collection which celebrates the joyfulness of Clare's writing, the sharpness of his eye and his knowledge and love of nature. Our title comes from the poem 'The Meadow Hay', where Clare describes his delight in observing the natural world. In it he becomes one with the weeds among which he lies, and his voice becomes the voice of the land itself.

The Meadow Hay

I often roam a minute from the path
Just to luxuriate on the new-mown swath,
And stretch me at my idle length along,
Hum louder o'er some melody or song
While passing stranger slackens in his pace
And turns to wonder what can haunt the place,
Unthinking that an idle rhymester lies
Buried in the sweet grass and feeding fantasies.
This happy spirit of the joyous day
Stirs every pulse of life into the play
Of buoyant joy and ecstasy – I walk
And hear the very weeds to sing and talk
Of their delights as the delighted wind
Toys with them like playfellows ever kind.

At first we had the bright idea that we could represent Clare's joyful side by printing all his poems which begin with the words 'I love'. That is indeed a frequent opening, and we found nearly fifty examples, and there were many others which, if they did not use those exact words, certainly continued the idea. But the resulting collection was in danger of being too repetitive and did not carry that wide-ranging passionate love of the natural world which we wished to represent; so we went back to the drawing board, although that original plan explains the number of 'I love' poems which we still include.

Our principles of selection have been few: to represent the joyful Clare; to avoid repetition of those poems included in *The Wood is Sweet,* to which we see this as a companion volume; and not to include the longer poems, or any fragments of longer poems except the brief claim to his right to song from 'The Progress of Rhyme'.

We have divided the poems into six sections, although it is evident that one cannot be dogmatic and rigid about divisions in Clare; he hated fences, and our groupings are merely loose gatherings.

The first section 'The Poet in the Fields' continues the theme of the title poem in exploring Clare's intimate involvement with nature, seeing no boundaries between himself, his poems, and the natural world in which he takes delight.

The subsequent sections gather together poems which respond to different aspects of that world. First is a section on flowers; though it is striking that for Clare 'flowers' did not mean showy garden plants but often the weeds which grew unnoticed and otherwise unsung in the land he knew: thistles, violets, ragwort, fern or the blossom of beans.

Then we have a section of poems on woods, those places to which Clare loved to retreat. As he says in 'The Woods', 'I seem to be myself / The only one that treads / The earth at such a time'. They provided him with peace, solitude, and the precious freedom to observe, of which he took full advantage.

Important among the things he observed there, and indeed everywhere he went, were the birds, and here again his preference is not for showy plumage and song, but for common birds. As he asks in 'The Wren': 'Why is the cuckoo's melody preferred / And nightingale's rich song so fondly praised / In poets' rhymes. Is there no other bird / Of nature's minstrelsy that oft hath raised / One's heart to ecstasy and mirth as well?' Clare's interest was in all birds, and some which we find rare and exotic were in fact common in his day. His attention to the bird life around him provides valuable evidence of the decline in numbers.

With his deep curiosity about the life around him, he was conscious of the changing aspects of the year, and so we have a series of poems on the seasons, which recognize that 'The seasons each as God bestows / Are simple and sublime'. There was always something that his eager eye found worthy of note and affection.

Clare's natural world is not static and prettified. It included the workers on the land, and his landscape is full of ploughboys, hedgers, haymakers, herdsmen, milkmaids; the whole village community whose daily lives had such intimate contact with the land. And it is Clare's hymn to the spirit of that land with which we end, his song 'To the Rural Muse', the inspiration of his verse, to which he cannot bid farewell.

Carry Akroyd's linocuts, which grace this book, are not so much illustrations of the poems as parallel evocations of the countryside, which take a hint from Clare and interpret it in her distinctive way, which aptly matches the quiet drama of the verse.

We should also say that the text has been lightly edited, mainly by adding punctuation and normalizing the spelling, and giving capital letters to the months and seasons but not to the birds. Subject/verb agreement has not been insisted on, and we have tried to retain Clare's dialectal character, which meant that we needed a brief glossary. We have given titles to some of the previously untitled poems.

R. K. R. Thornton

CHRONOLGY

1793	Born 13 July in Helpston, son of poor peasants Parker Clare and his wife Ann. A twin sister, Bessy, dies soon after.
1798	Wordsworth and Coleridge's *Lyrical Ballads*. His only surviving sibling, his sister Sophy is born (d.1855)
1800s	Brief schooling at Helpston and Glinton. Meets Mary Joyce (relationship continues until c.1815-16).
	A variety of casual jobs: pot-boy, gardener at Burghley House.
1806	Inspired by reading Thomson's *The Seasons*, begins to write poetry
1809	Works as pot boy at the Blue Bell Inn, Helpston
1812	Brief period in the militia
1814	Buys his blank book from J. B. Henson, a bookseller in Market Deeping
1817	Father disabled by rheumatism. Works as a lime burner at Bridge Casterton to help with the family finances.
1818-19	Henson prints proposals for publishing Clare's poems. Meets Edward Drury and through him John Taylor, the London publisher.
1820	*Poems Descriptive of Rural Life and Scenery* (January), goes into four editions by 1821. Visits to Burghley House and Milton Park, homes of the local aristocracy.
	Visits London (March). His portrait is painted by William Hilton.
	Marries on 16 March Martha (Patty) Turner (1799-1871)
	Daughter Anna Maria born (2 June)

1821	*The Village Minstrel, and Other Poems* (September)
1821	Death of Keats (b.1795). Birth and death of a son.
1822	Death of Shelley (b.1792). Clare's second visit to London; meets Lamb, Hazlitt, de Quincey, and Cary at headquarters of *London Magazine*
1823	Planning begins for next book. Long period of illness.
1824	Death of Byron (b.1788); Clare is in London and sees his cortège
1827	*The Shepherd's Calendar* (April)
1827	Death of Blake (b. 1757)
1828	Last visit to London
1830	More severe illness
1832	Moves from cottage of his birth to Northborough
1834	Death of Coleridge (b.1834)
1835	*The Rural Muse* (July). Death of his mother.
1837	Goes to Dr. Matthew Allen's asylum at High Beech in Epping Forest
1838	Death of Mary Joyce
1841	Walks from Essex to Northborough (July)
1841	Enters Northampton General Lunatic Asylum (Dec)
1846	Death of Parker Clare, John Clare's father
1850	Death of Wordsworth (b.1770)
1864	Dies on 20 May in Northampton; buried in Helpston on the 25th.

THE POET IN THE FIELDS

SONG'S ETERNITY

What is song's eternity?
Come and see.
Can it noise and bustle be?
Come and see.
Praises sung or praises said
Can it be?
Wait awhile and these are dead –
Sigh, sigh –
Be they high or lowly bred,
They die.

What is song's eternity?
Come and see
Melodies of earth and sky,
Here they be:
Songs once sung to Adam's ears
Can it be?
Ballads of six thousand years
Thrive, thrive;
Songs awakened with the spheres
Alive.

Mighty songs that miss decay,
What are they?
Crowds and cities pass away
Like a day;
Books are writ and books are read;
What are they?

Years will lay them with the dead –
Sigh, sigh –
Trifles unto nothing wed,
They die.

Dreamers, list the honey bee;
Mark the tree
Where the blue cap – tootle tee –
Sings a glee
Sung to Adam and to Eve;
Here they be.
When floods covered every bough
Noah's ark
Heard that ballad singing now;
Hark, hark.

Tootle tootle tootle tee;
Can it be
Pride and fame must shadows be?
Come and see
Every season own her own,
Bird and bee
Sing creation's music on;
Nature's glee
Is in every mood and tone
Eternity.

The eternity of song
Liveth here.
Nature's universal tongue
Singeth here
Songs I've heard and felt and seen
Everywhere;
Songs like the grass are evergreen;
The giver
Said live and be, and they have been
For ever.

RURAL SCENES

I never saw a man in all my days –
One whom the calm of quietness pervades –
Who gave not woods and fields his hearty praise,
And felt a happiness in Summer shades.
There I meet common thoughts, that all may read
Who love the quiet fields: – I note them well,
Because they give me joy as I proceed,
And joy renewed, when I their beauties tell
In simple verse, and unambitious songs,
That in some mossy cottage haply may
Be read, and win the praise of humble tongues
In the green shadows of some after-day.
For rural fame may likeliest rapture yield
To hearts, whose songs are gathered from the field.

FROM 'THE PROGRESS OF RHYME'

I felt that I'd a right to song
And sung – but in a timid strain
Of fondness for my native plain.
For every thing I felt a love,
The weeds below, the birds above
And weeds that bloomed in Summer's hours
I thought they should be reckoned flowers;
They made a garden free for all
And so I loved them great and small
And sung of some that pleased my eye
Nor could I pass the thistle by
But paused and thought it could not be
A weed in nature's poesy. . . .
And so it cheered me while I lay
Among their beautiful array
To think that I in humble dress
Might have a right to happiness.

STONE PIT

The passing traveller with wonder sees
A deep and ancient stone pit full of trees;
So deep and very deep the place has been
The church might stand within and not be seen.
The passing stranger oft with wonder stops
And thinks he e'en could walk upon their tops
And often stoops to see the busy crow
And stands above and sees the eggs below;
And while the wild horse gives his head a toss
The squirrel dances up and runs across.
The boy that stands and kills the black-nosed bee
Dares down as soon as magpies' nests are found
And wonders when he climbs the highest tree
To find it reaches scarce above the ground.

SABBATH BELLS

I've often on a sabbath day,
Where pastoral quiet dwells,
Lay down among the new mown hay
To listen distant bells
That beautifully flung the sound
Upon the quiet wind
While beans in blossom breathed around
A fragrance o'er the mind;

A fragrance and a joy beside
That never wears away.
The very air seems deified
Upon a sabbath day;
So beautiful the flitting wrack
Slow pausing from the eye;
Earth's music seemed to call them back,
Calm settled in the sky.

And I have listened till I felt
A feeling not in words,
A love that rudest moods would melt
When those sweet sounds was heard;
A melancholy joy at rest,
A pleasurable pain,
A love, a rapture of the breast
That nothing will explain:

A dream of beauty that displays
Imaginary joys
That all the world in all its ways
Finds not to realize.
All idly stretched upon the hay,
The wind flirt fanning by,
How soft, how sweetly swept away
The music of the sky.

The ear it lost and caught the sound;
Swelled beautifully on
A fitful melody around
Of sweetness heard and gone.
I felt such thoughts I yearned to sing
The humming air's delight
That seemed to move the swallow's wing
Into a wilder flight.

The butterfly in wings of brown
Would find me where I lay,
Fluttering and bobbing up and down
And settling on the hay.
The waving blossoms seemed to throw
Their fragrance to the sound
While up and down and loud and low
The bells were ringing round.

AN IDLE HOUR

Sauntering at ease I often love to lean
O'er old bridge walls and mark the flood below
Whose ripples through the weeds of oily green
Like happy travellers mutter as they go,
And mark the sunshine dancing on the arch
Time keeping to the merry waves beneath,
And on the banks see drooping blossoms parch,
Thirsting for water in the day's hot breath,
Right glad of mud drops plashed upon their leaves
By cattle plunging from the steepy brink,
While water flowers more than their share receive
And revel to their very cups in drink;
Just like the world some strive and fare but ill
While others riot and have plenty still.

A SEAT IN THE MEADOWS

I love to stroll the meadow when it's mown
And all the crowd of luscious scented hay
Is cleared away and left the sward alone
Beneath the quiet of a lovely day;
And there I love green leisure to delay
Beside some lake to find a pleasant seat,
To sit luxuriantly in danger's way
And almost let the water touch my feet.
A something so refreshing, bland and cool
From the calm surface of the water steals
What time the noontide spangles o'er the pool
Bringing back bits of joy past time conceals
And youth's past visions flit across the brain,
What books nor pictures never meet again.

THE PASTURE

The pewet is come to the green
And swops o'er the swain at his plough
Where the green sward in places is seen
Pressed down by the lairs of the cow;
The mole roots her hillocks anew
For seasons to dress at their wills
In their thyme and their beautiful dew;
For the pasture's delight is its hills.

They invite us when weary to drop
On their cushions awhile – and again
They invite us when musing to stop
And see how they checker the plain;
And the old hills swell out in the sun
So inviting e'en now – that the boy
Has his game of peg morris begun
And cuts his rude figures in joy.

When I stroll o'er the molehilly green,
Stepping onward from hillock to hill,
I think over pictures I've seen
And feel them deliciously still.
I think when the glad shepherd lay
On the velvet sward stretched for a bed
On the bosom of sunshiney May
While an hillock supported his head.

I think, when in weeding, the maid
Made choice of a hill for her seat
When the winds so deliciously played
In her curls 'mid her blushes so sweet;
I think of gay groups in the shade
In hay time with noise never still
When the short sward their gay cushions made
And their dinner was spread on a hill.

I think when in harvest folks lay
Underneath the green shade of a tree
While the childern were busy at play
Running round the huge trunk in their glee.
Joy shouted wherever I went
And e'en now such a freshness it yields
I could fancy with books and a tent
What delight we could find in the fields.

THE HEATH

How I love the dear wild and the desolate heath
With its sweet swelling uplands and downs,
When I toil up the path till I'm half out of breath
While the oak wood the distance embrowns

With the first hues of Spring – and the mossy thorn tree
Shines in its most delicate hue,
And the long withered grass reaching up to my knee
Rustles loud as my feet brushes through.

Where the furze on the slopes burn from green into gold
With their millions of blossoms and ling
Blushing red underneath is most sweet to behold
Where the wood lark sits pruning her wing.

Such a freshness comes round from the wide spreading air,
Such a smell from the blossoms beneath,
Such a beautiful something refreshes me there
While I ramble about on the heath.

The old hills that for a man's lifetime hath stood
Unmolested 'mid bushes and burrs;
The wagon ways leading along to the wood
And the rabbit tracks into the furze.

There nought but a shepherd cries 'whoop' to his sheep
Or a herdsman hails 'hoi' to his cows
And the noise of the wagoner trailing the steep
While crossing the pudges and sloughs,

Oft standing to rest them and then with a smack
Of his whip driving onward again
While the wood in an echo repeateth the crack
And the load of wood creaks on the wain.

Though simple to some I delight in the sight
Of such objects that bring unto me
A picture of picturesque joy and delight
Where beauty and harmony be.

O I love at my heart to be strolling along
O'er the heath a new impulse to find
While I hum to the wind in a ballad or song
Some fancy that starts in the mind.

All seem so delightful and bring to the mind
Such quiet and beautiful joys
That the mind when it's weary like hermits may find
A retreat from earth's follies and noise.

EMMONSAILS HEATH IN WINTER

I love to see the old heath's withered brake
Mingle its crimpled leaves with furze and ling,
While the old heron from the lonely lake
Starts slow and flaps his melancholy wing,
And oddling crow in idle motions swing
On the half rotten ash tree's topmost twig,
Beside whose trunk the gipsy makes his bed.
Up flies the bouncing woodcock from the brig
Where a black quagmire quakes beneath the tread,
The fieldfares chatters in the whistling thorn
And for the haw round fields and closen rove,
And coy bumbarrels twenty in a drove
Flit down the hedgerows in the frozen plain
And hang on little twigs and start again.

CARELESS RAMBLES

I love to wander at my idle will
In Summer's luscious prime about the fields
And kneel when thirsty at the little rill
To sip the draught its pebbly bottom yields,
And, where the maple bush its fountain shields,
To lie and rest a swaily hour away
And crop the swelling peasecod from the land
Or 'mid the upland's woodland walks to stray
Where oaks for aye o'er their old shadows stand
'Neath whose dark foliage with a welcome hand
I pluck the luscious strawberry ripe and red
As beauty's lips – and in my fancy's dreams,
As 'mid the velvet moss I musing tread,
Feel life as lovely as her picture seems.

EVENING

It is the silent hour when they who roam
    Seek shelter, on the earth or ocean's breast;
It is the hour when travel finds a home,
    On deserts, or within the cot to rest.
    It is the hour when joy and grief are blest,
And Nature finds repose where'er she roves;
    It is the hour that lovers like the best,
When in the twilight shades or darker groves
The maiden wanders with the swain she loves;

The balmy hour when fond hearts fondly meet;
    The hour when dew like welcome rest descends
On wild-flowers, shedding forth their odours sweet;
    The hour when sleep lays foes as quiet friends;
    The hour when labour's toilworn journey ends,
And seeks the cot for sweet repose till morn;
    The hour when prayer from all to God ascends;
At twilight's hour love's softest sighs are born,
When lovers linger 'neath the flowering thorn.

Oh! at this hour I love to be abroad,
    Gazing upon the moonlit scene around,
'Looking through Nature up to Nature's God',[1]
    Regarding all with reverence profound!
    The wild flowers studding every inch of ground,
And trees, with dews bespangled, looking bright
    As burnished silver; – while the entrancing sound
Of melody, from the sweet bird of night,
Fills my whole soul with rapture and delight.

---

[1] The quotation is from Alexander Pope's *Essay on Man.*

FLOWERS

THE POESY OF FLOWERS

What would the rosey be but as the rose?
A merely sweet undignifying flower;
But clothed by woman's dignifying grace
It looks upon us with a living power;
Then quickly every blush from beauty glows
As mirrors – there reflecting beauty's face;
Her lips and luscious cheeks shine in its leaves
And in the lily – there her bosom heaves.
Flowers thus personify the heart's delight
And beauty gives us rapture in their sight.
Flowers merely flowers would seem but cold esteems
With heart-associations and love-dreams
But mixed like life with mind, where'er we roam
They link like household feelings with our home.

WOOD ANEMONE

The wood anemone through dead oak leaves
And in the thickest woods now blooms anew
And where the green briar, and the bramble weaves
Thick clumps o' green, anemones thicker grew
And weeping flowers, in thousands pearled in dew
People the woods and brakes' hid hollows there –
White, yellow and purple hued the wide wood through.
What pretty, drooping weeping flowers they are;
The clipped frilled leaves, the slender stalk they bear
On which the drooping flower hangs weeping dew.
How beautiful through April time and May
The woods look, filled with wild anemone
And every little spinney now looks gay
With flowers 'mid brush wood and the huge oak tree.

THE PRIMROSE

Welcome pale primrose, starting up between
Dead matted leaves of ash and oak that strew
The every lawn, the wood and spinney through,
'Mid creeping moss and ivy's darker green;
How much thy presence beautifies the ground.
How bright thy modest unaffected pride
Glows on the sunny bank and woodland side
And where thy fairy flowers in groups are found
The school-boy roams enchantedly along
Plucking the fairest with a rude delight,
And the meek shepherd stops his simple song
To gaze a moment on the pleasing sight,
O'erjoyed to see the flowers that truly bring
The welcome news of soft returning Spring.

PRIMROSES

I love the rathe primroses, pale brimstone primroses
    That bloom in the thick wood and i' the green closes;
I love the primroses whenever they come,
    Where the blue fly sits pensive and humble bees hum.
The pale brimstone primroses come at the Spring,
    Swept over and fanned by the wild thrush's wing,
Bowed down to the leaf-covered ground by the bees
    Who sing their Spring ballads through bushes and trees

Like patches o' flame i' the Ivy so green
    And dark green oak leaves where the Autumn has been.
Put on thy straw hat, love, and russet stuff gown
    And see the pale primroses grow up and down,
The pale brimstone primroses, wild wood primroses,
    Which maids i' the dark woods make into posies.
Put on thy stuff gown, love, and off let us be
    To seek brimstone primroses 'neath the Oak tree.

Spring time is come, love, primroses bloom fair.
    The sun o' the morning shines in thy bright hair.
The ancient wood shadows are bonny dark green
    That throw out like giants the stovens between;
While brimstone primroses like patches o' flame
    Blaze through the dead leaves making Ivy look tame.
I love the rathe primrose in hedgerows and closes.
    Together let's wander to gather primroses.

TO THE VIOLET

Hail to thee violet, sweet careless spread
'Neath each warm bush and covert budding hedge.
In many a pleasing walk have I been led
To seek thee – promise of Spring's earliest pledge,
In modest coyness hanging down its head
Unconscious hiding beauties from the eye
And sweetly brooding o'er its graceful form,
Shunning each vulgar gaze that saunters by
And timely stooping from an April storm,
As virtue startled by approaching harm
Shrinks from delusion's false betraying hands,
With bashful look that more the bosom warms.
So sweetest blossom the coy violet stands
Tempting the plunderer with a double charm.

MARCH VIOLET

Where last year's leaves and weeds decay
March violets are in blow;
I'd rake the rubbish all away
And give them room to grow.

Near neighbour to the arum proud
Where dew drops fall and sleep;
As purple as a fallen cloud,
March violets bloom and creep.

Scenting the gales of early morn,
They smell before they're seen,
Peeping beneath the old whitethorn
That shows its tender green.

The lambs will nibble by their bloom
And eat them day by day
Till briars forbid his steps to come
And then he skips away.

Mid nettle stalks that wither there
And on the greensward lie
All bleaching in the thin march air
The scattered violets lie.

I know the place; it is a place
In Spring where nettles come;
There milk white violets show their face
And blue ones earlier bloom.

THE COWSLIPS

The dancing cowslips come in pleasant hours;
Though seldom sung, they're everybody's flowers:
They hurry from the world, and leave the cold;
And all the meadows turn from green to gold:
The shepherd finds them where he went to play,
And wears a nosegay in his mouth all day:
The maiden finds them in the pleasant grove,
And puts them in her bosom with her love;
She loves the ladysmocks: and just beyond
The water blobs close to the meadow-pond.
I've often gone about where blackthorns stood
And got the Bedlam-cowslips in the wood;
Then found the blackbird's nest, and noisy jay
And up and threw the cowslips all away!

THE RAGWORT

Ragwort thou humble flower with tattered leaves,
I love to see thee come and litter gold,
What time the Summer binds her russet sheaves,
Decking rude spots in beauties manifold
That without thee were dreary to behold,
Sunburnt and bare – the meadow bank, the baulk
That leads a wagonway through mellow fields
Rich with the tints that harvest's plenty yields,
Browns of all hues – and everywhere I walk
Thy waste of shining blossoms richly shields
The sun tanned sward in splendid hues that burn
So bright and glaring that the very light
Of the rich sunshine doth to paleness turn
And seems but very shadows in thy sight.

THISTLES

Where the broad sheep walk bare and brown
With scant grass pining after showers
And winds go fanning up and down
The little strawy bents and nodding flowers,
There the huge thistle spurred with many thorns
The suncracked uplands' russet swells adorns.

Not undevoid of beauty, there they come,
Armed warriors waiting neither suns nor showers,
Guarding the little clover plats to bloom
While sheep nor oxen dare not crop their flowers,
Unsheathing their own knobs of tawny flowers
When Summer cometh in her hottest hours.

The pewet swopping up and down
And screaming round the passer by
Or running o'er the herbage brown
With copple crown uplifted high
Loves in its clumps to make a home
Where danger seldom cares to come.

The yellow hammer often pressed
For spot to build and be unseen
Will in its shelter trust her nest
When fields and meadows glow with green,
And larks, though paths go closely by,
Will in its shade securely lie.

The partridge too that scarce can trust
The open downs to be at rest
Will in its clumps lie down and dust
And prune its horseshoe circled breast
And often shunning fields of green
Will lay and raise its brood unseen.

The sheep when hunger presses sore
May nip the clover round its nest
But soon the thistle wounding sore
Relieves it from each brushing guest
That leaves a bit of wool behind
The yellow hammer loves to find.

The horse will set his foot and bite
Close to the ground lark's guarded nest
And snort to meet the prickly sight
That fans the feathers of her breast,
Yet thistles prick so deep that he
Turns back and leaves her dwelling free.

Its prickly knobs the dews of morn
Doth bead with dressing rich to see
When threads doth hang from thorn to thorn
Like the small spinner's tapestry
And from the flowers a sultry smell
Comes that agrees with summer well.

The bee will make its bloom a bed,
The bumble bee in tawny brown,
And one in jacket fringed with red
Will rest upon its velvet down
When overtaken in the rain
And wait till sunshine comes again.

And there are times when travel goes
Along the sheep tracks' beaten ways
That pleasure many a praise bestows
Upon its blossom's pointed rays
When other things are parched beside
And hot days leaves it in its pride.

THE THISTLE

I love the thistle with its ruddy flowers;
It cheers me on the waste in lonely hours;
It cheers me in lone sunshine out of doors
When seeking solitude on rushy moors;
It cheers me resting on the way-side stones
Where tears of morning glitter on the thorns.
I love the thistle, 'tis an ill-used flower
And bees are singing round for many an hour.

I love the thistle and its prickles too.
Cobwebs are round it with a veil of dew.
I love the thistle where it bravely stands
For rights of Liberty in many lands,
Simply defying every roguish eye
With 'wha dare meddle wi me' that passes by:
My right is simple, blooming 'mong the flowers
That God's hand scatters on this land of ours.

So I love the thistles spread round Scottish bowers;
Better than any other of the wildling flowers
I love the warrior thistle where it stands,
Though often wounded in the legs and hands.
On Bannockburn its bloom undaunted stood,
Dyed deeper in the streams of human blood.

THE CLUMP OF FERN

Pleasures lie scattered all about our ways,
Harvest for thought and joy to look and glean;
Much of the beautiful to win our praise
Lie where we never heeded aught had been.
By this wood stile half buried in the shade
Of rude disorder – bramble, woodbine, all
So thickly wove that nutters scarcely made
An entrance through – and, now the acorns fall,
The gatherers seeking entrance pause awhile
Ere they mount up the bank to climb the stile,
Half wishing that a better road was nigh;
Yet here 'mid leaf-strewn morning's Autumn mild
While pleasing sounds and pleasing sights are by
Things beautiful delight my heart to smile.

Here underneath the stile's moss-covered post
A little bunch of fern doth thrive and spring,
Hid from the noisy wind and coming frost
Like late reared young 'neath the wood pigeon's wing.
I've seen beneath the furze bush clumps of ling
So beautiful in pinky knots of bloom
That made the inmost heart's emotions breathe
A favourite love for the unsocial heath,
That gives man no inviting hopes to come
To fix his dwelling and disturb the scene.
So in my loneliness of mood this green
Large clump of crimpled fern leaves doth bequeath
Like feelings – and whenever wanderers roam
Some little scraps of happiness is seen.

THE BEANS IN BLOSSOM

The southwest wind how pleasant in the face
It breathes while, sauntering in a musing pace,
I roam these new ploughed fields and by the side
Of this old wood where happy birds abide
And the rich blackbird through his golden bill
Utters wild music when the rest are still.
Now luscious comes the scent of blossomed beans
That o'er the path in rich disorder leans,
'Mid which the bees in busy songs and toils
Load home luxuriantly their yellow spoils.
The herd cows toss the mole hills in their play
And often stand the stranger's steps at bay,
'Mid clover blossoms red and tawny white,
Strong scented with the summer's warm delight.

FORESTS, WOODS AND TREES

A WALK IN THE FOREST

I love the forest and its airy bounds,
Where friendly Campbell takes his daily rounds;
I love the break neck hills, that headlong go,
And leave me high, and half the world below;
I love to see the Beach Hill mounting high,
The brook without a bridge, and nearly dry.
There's Bucket's Hill, a place of furze and clouds,
Which evening in a golden blaze enshrouds:
I hear the cows go home with tinkling bell,
And see the woodman in the forest dwell,
Whose dog runs eager where the rabbit's gone;
He eats the grass, then kicks and hurries on;
Then scrapes for hoarded bone, and tries to play,
And barks at larger dogs and runs away.

THE FOREST MAID

I love to see the forest maid
    Go in the pleasant day,
And jump to break an idle bough
    To drive the flies away.

Her face is brown with open air,
    And like the lily blooming;
But beauty, whether brown or fair,
    Is always found with women!

She stooped to tie her pattens up,
    And showed a cleanly stocking;
The flowers made curtsies all the way,
    Against her ankles knocking.

She stooped to get the foxglove bells
    That grew among the bushes,
And, careless, set her basket down,
    And tied them up with rushes.

Her face was ever in a smile,
    And brown, and softly blooming;
I often met the scorn of man,
    But welcome lives with woman!

THE WIND AND TREES

I love the song of tree and wind,
How beautiful they sing.
The lichen on the beach tree rind
E'en beats the flowers of Spring.

From the southwest, sugh, sugh it comes
Then whizzes round in pleasant hums;
It sings the spirit of the storm.
The trees with dancing waxes warm;

They dance and bow, and dance again,
The very trunks, each branch and grain
Shake and dance and wave and bow
In every form no matter how.

In every storm they dance on high,
The semblance of a stormy sky,
Then sob and roar and bend and swee,
The semblance of a stormy sea.

I love the song of wood and wind,
The sobs before, its roar behind.
I love the stir of flood and tree;
'Tis all of nature's melody.

I love the roaring of the wind;
The calm that follows cheers the mind.
'Tis like the good man's end of peace
When joys begin and troubles cease.

WINDY DAYS

Summer is on the earth and in the sky,
The days all sunny and the fields all green;
The woods spread o'er the hills a canopy
Of beauty's harmony in every scene.
Like to a map the fields and valleys lie.
Winds dash in wildest motions the woods' green
And every wave of leaves and every billow
Lies in the sun like Beauty on a pillow.

There is a freshness in the leafy sprays
That dashes o'er the forest from the wind,
The wild sublimity of windy days
Like the rich thinkings of a master mind,
Or dashes on the canvas none can find
In works inferior – when the woods all blaze
With a wild sunset and the winds unbind
Their foliage to the heaven's wild amaze,
Field, meadow, wood rolling o'er stormy days.

The roaring of the woods is like a sea,
All thunder and commotion to the shore.
The old oaks toss their branches to be free
And urge the fury of the storm the more.
Louder than thunder is the sobbing roar
Of leafy billows to their shore, the sky,
Round which the bloodshot clouds like fields of gore
In angry silence did at anchor lie
As if the battle's roar was not yet by.

Anon the wind has ceased, the woods are still;
The winds are sobbed to sleep and all is rest;
The clouds like solid rocks too jagged for hills
Lie quietly ashore upon the west.
The cottage ceases rocking – each tired guest
Sleeps sounder for the heavy storm's uproar.
– How calm the sunset blazes in the west
As if the waking storm would burst no more
And this still even seems more calmer than before.

THE WOODS

I love to roam the woods,
Oft patted by the boughs
That meet from either side
And form an arch of leaves
Till, hidden as it were from all the world,
I stand and muse upon the pleasant scene.

I seem to be my self
The only one that treads
The earth at such a time,
So vacant is the mass
That spreads around me one huge sea of leaves
And intertwining grains of thickest shades.

No human eye is visible,
No human sound attracts
The ear – but musing solitude,
One unembodied thought,
Thinks the heart into stillness as the world
Was left behind for something green and new

And lonely – and I've thought
In such a spot to build
An hermitage or hut
With books and leisure left.
How sweet t'would be, but then again
I've turned to my old home and felt it vain.

Yet sure a hut close thatched,
Chafed by o'erhanging boughs
In such a place when night
Dark on the crowd of trees
Found us locked in beside a blazing fire
Might give us happiness and pleasing fears:

Fear books can give us
When we read strange tales
Of dwellers in the depths
Of earth's untrodden shades
Where woods surround lone huts impassable
And nought lives near them but the hope of heaven.

TO THE WINDS

Hail gentle winds, I love your murmuring sounds;
The willows charm me wavering to and fro
And oft I stretch me on the daisied ground
To see you crimp the wrinkling flood below,
Delighted more as brisker gusts succeed
And give the landscape around a sweeter grace,
Sweeping in shaded waves the ripening mead,
Puffing their rifled fragrance in my face.
Pictures of nature, ye are doubly dear;
Her childern dearly love your whispering charms.
Ah, ye have murmured sweet to many an ear
That now lies dormant in death's icy arms;
And at this moment many a weed ye want
That hides the bard in his forgotten grave.

THE OLD WILLOW

The juicey wheat now spindles into ear
And trailing pea blooms ope their velvet eyes
And weeds and flowers by crowds far off and near
In all their sunny liveries appear
For Summer's lustre boasts unnumbered dyes.
How pleasant 'neath this willow by the brook
That's kept its ancient place for many a year
To sit and o'er these crowded fields to look
And the soft dropping of the shower to hear;
Ourselves so sheltered, e'en a pleasant book
Might lie uninjured from the fragrant rain,
For not a drop gets through the bowering leaves
But, dry as housed in my old hut again,
I sit and troublous care of half its claim deceive.

I LOVE TO WANDER BY THE IVY BANK

I love to wander by the ivy bank
Where schoolboys gather pooties and where drank
The wood man toiling in the morning mirk
The dribbling dyke and went again to work.
Bird nesters wandering far away from home
Pulled up the teazle burrs and called them combs
And in short bushes where the cattle browse
They pulled the docks and called them milking cows;
Where saucy boys that in the rushes lie
Has saucy words for all that passes by.
I love the ivy bank to wander by
And see the rotten sticks on bushes lie
And hear among the oaks the wood man's knocks,
The howling badger and the barking fox.

THE HAWTHORN

I love the hawthorn well –
The first green thing
In woods and hedges – blackthorn dell
Dashed with its green first Spring
When sallows shine in golden sheen,
These white thorn places in the black, how green!

How beautifully green
Though March has but begun
To tend primroses planted in the sun;
The roots that's further in
Are not begun to bud or may be just begun.

I love the white thorn bough
Hung over the mole hill
Where the Spring feeding cow
Rubs off the dew drop chill,
When on the cowslip peeps and glossy thorn
The dews hang shining pearls at early morn.

A HAWTHORN NOOK

The smooth and velvet sward my fancy suits
In pleasant places where the hawthorns look
As left for arbours, and the old tree roots
Lie cramped and netted o'er the guggling brook
And shepherd on his elbow lolls to read
His slips of ballads bought at neighbouring fair,
Seeming unconscious of the beauties there:
The stilly quiet of the grassy screed
Skirting the busy brook – the happy fare
Of little birds that in the bushes breed
Are all unnoticed save that careless way
That sees and feels not. There I love to pass
The green hours' leisure in a Summer's day,
Stretching at length upon the couching grass.

BIRDS

SAND MARTIN

Thou hermit haunter of the lonely glen
And common wild and heath – the desolate face
Of rude waste landscapes far away from men
Where frequent quarries give thee dwelling place,
With strangest taste and labour undeterred
Drilling small holes along the quarry's side,
More like the haunts of vermin than a bird
And seldom by the nesting boy descried.
I've seen thee far away from all thy tribe
Flirting about the unfrequented sky
And felt a feeling that I can't describe
Of lone seclusion and a hermit joy
To see thee circle round nor go beyond
That lone heath and its melancholy pond.

THE WREN

Why is the cuckoo's melody preferred
And nightingale's rich song so fondly praised
In poets' rhymes? Is there no other bird
Of nature's minstrelsy that oft hath raised
One's heart to ecstasy and mirth as well?
I judge not how another's taste is caught;
With mine there's other birds that bear the bell
Whose song hath crowds of happy memories brought.
Such the wood robin singing in the dell
And little wren that many a time hath sought
Shelter from showers in huts where 1 did dwell
In early Spring, the tenant of the plain,
Tenting my sheep; and still they come to tell
The happy stories of the past again.

THE MARCH NIGHTINGALE

Now sallow catkins, once all downy white,
Turn like the sunshine into golden light;
The rocking clown leans o'er the spinney rail
In admiration at the sunny sight;
The while the blackcap doth his ears assail
With such a rich and such an early song
He stops his own and thinks the nightingale
Hath of her monthly reckoning counted wrong.
'Sweet jug jug jug' comes loud upon his ear –
Those sounds that unto May by right belong –
Yet on the hawthorn scarce a leaf appears;
How can it be? Spell-struck the wondering boy
Listens again – again the sound he hears
And mocks it in his song for very joy.

THE NIGHTINGALE

This is the month the nightingale, clod-brown,
    Is heard among the woodland shady boughs;
This is the time when in the vale grass-grown
    The maiden hears at eve her lover's vows,
    What time the blue mist, round her patient cows,
Dim rises from the grass, and half conceals
    Their dappled hides. I hear the nightingale,
That from the little blackthorn spinny steals
    To the old hazel hedge that skirts the vale,
And still unseen sings sweet. The ploughman feels
    The thrilling music as he goes along,
And imitates and listens, – while the fields
    Lose all their paths in dusk, to lead him wrong,
    Still sings the nightingale her sweet melodious song.

LARKS AND SPRING

The sunny end of March is nigh
And not a cloud is in the sky;
Along the footpath o'er the farm
The school-boy, basket on his arm,
Seeks the bird's nest, therein to look.
He takes a stone to cross the brook
Made wider by the rainy night
And hums the music of delight
To see the rabbits seek their burrow,
Or ground lark from the fallowed furrow
Start up and shiver while he sings
Then drop as though he'd lost his wings
As stunt and heavy as a stone
In the brown furrow still and lone.
And still I love the ground-lark's flight,
Starting up the ploughman's height,
And more and more unseal his eye
When rose leaves pave the eastern sky

To see the skylark as he springs
Shake morning's moisture from his wings
And rise and sing in music proud,
Small as a bee beneath a cloud,
'Till mixing with the vapours dun
He's lost in valleys of the sun;
And singing on in Spring's delight
Some moments ere he comes in sight
It drops, and drops from breezy morn
To seek its mate amid the corn.
A happy song the skylark brings
And Spring's in every note he sings.
With coppled crown, and speckled breast;
The pilewort blooms above his nest.
In rain it seeks the sheltering furrow
But sings when sunshine comes tomorrow.
In every field they mount and sing
The songs of Nature and of Spring.

THE SKYLARK LEAVING HER NEST

Right happy bird so full of mirth,
Mounting and mounting still more high
To meet morn's sunshine in the sky
Ere yet it smiles on earth;

How often I delight to stand,
Listening a minute's length away
Where Summer spreads her green array
By wheat or barley land,

To see thee with a sudden start
The green and placid herbage leave
And in mid air a vision weave
For joy's delighted heart,

Shedding to heaven a vagrant mirth
When silence husheth other themes
And woods in their dark splendour dreams
Like heaviness on earth.

My mind enjoys the happy sight
To watch thee to the clear blue sky
And when I downward turn my eye
Earth glows with lonely light.

Then nearer comes thy happy sounds
And downward drops thy little wing
And now the valleys hear thee sing
And all the dewy grounds

Gleam into joy now from the eye;
Thou'rt dropping sudden as a stone
And now thou'rt in the wheat alone
And still the circle of the sky,

And absent like a pleasure gone.
Though many come within the way
Thy little song to peeping day
Is still remembered on.

For who that crosses fields of corn
Where skylarks start to meet the day
But feels more pleasure on his way
Upon a Summer's morn.

'Tis one of those heart-cheering sights
In green earth's rural chronicles
That upon every memory dwells
Among home fed delights.

THE HAPPY BIRD

The happy whitethroat on the sweeing bough –
Swayed by the impulse of the gadding wind
That ushers in the showers of April – now
Singeth right joyously and, now reclined,
Croucheth and clingeth to her moving seat
To keep her hold; and, till the wind for rest
Pauses, she mutters inward melodies
That seem her heart's rich thinkings to repeat;
And when the branch is still, her little breast
Swells out in rapture's gushing symphonies
And then against her brown wing softly pressed
The wind comes playing, an enraptured guest.
This way and that she swees, till gusts arise
More boisterous in their play, and off she flies.

THE REED BIRD

A little slender bird of reddish brown
With frequent haste pops in and out the reeds
And on the river frequent flutters down
As if for food and so securely feeds
Her little young that in their ambush needs
Her frequent journeys, hid in thickest shade
Where danger never finds a path to show
A fear on comfort's nest securely made
In woods of reeds round which the waters flow,
Save by a jelted stone that boys will throw
Or passing rustle of the fisher's boat.
It is the reed bird prized for pleasant note,
A happy songster; man can seldom share
A spot so hidden from the haunts of care.

I LOVE TO HEAR THE EVENING CROWS GO BY

I love to hear the evening crows go by
And see the starnels darken down the sky;
The bleaching stack the bustling sparrow leaves
And plops with merry note beneath the eaves;
The odd and lated pigeon bounces by
As if a wary watching hawk was nigh,
While far and fearing nothing, high and slow,
The stranger birds to distant places go,
While short of flight the evening robin comes
To watch the maiden sweeping out the crumbs,
Nor fears the idle shout of passing boy
But pecks about the door and sings for joy;
Then in the hovel where the cows are fed
Finds till the morning comes a pleasant bed.

THE BLACKBIRD

The blackbird is a bonny bird
    That singeth in the wood;
His song is in the evening heard
    When the red cow chews her cud;
His song is heard in morning loud
    Upon the bright white thorn
While the blithe milkmaid sings as proud
    And holds the world in scorn.

O bonny is the blackbird still
    On top of yon fir tree
On which he wipes his golden bill
    And blithely whistles he;
He sings upon the sapling oak
    In notes all rich and mellow.
Oft have I quit town's noise, and folk
    In Spring's sweet Summer's weather.

The blackbird is a bonny bird;
    I love his mourning suit,
And song in the Spring mornings heard
    As mellow as the flute.
How sweet his song in April showers
    Pipes from his golden bill,
As yellow as the kingcup flowers,
    The sweetest ditty still.

THE CROW

How peaceable it seems for lonely men
To see a crow fly in the thin blue sky
Over the woods and fields, o'er level fen;
It speaks of villages, or cottage nigh
Behind the neighbouring woods.When March winds high
Tear off the branches of the huge old oak,
I love to see these chimney sweeps sail by
And hear them o'er the gnarled forest croak
Then sosh askew from the hid woodman's stroke
That in the woods their daily labours ply.
I love the sooty crow nor would provoke
Its March day exercise of croaking joy.
I love to see it sailing to and fro
While fields, and woods and waters spread below.

CROWS

The crow will tumble up and down
At the first sight of Spring
And in old trees around the town
Brush Winter from its wing.

No longer flapping far away,
To naked fen they fly;
Chill fare as on a Winter's day
But field and valleys nigh,

Where swains are stirring out to plough
And woods are just at hand,
They seek the upland's sunny brow
And strut from land to land

And often flap their sooty wing
And sturt to neighbouring tree
And seems to try all ways to sing
And almost speaks in glee.

The ploughman hears and turns his head
Above to wonder why
And there a new nest nearly made
Proclaims the Winter by.

The schoolboy free from Winter's frown
That rests on every stile
In wonder sets his basket down
To start his happy toil.

ROOKS NESTING

The rooks begin to build and pleasant looks
The homestead elms now almost black with rooks.
The birds at first for mastership will try;
They fight for sticks and squabble as they fly
And if a stranger comes they soon invade
And pull his nest in pieces soon as made;
The carrion crow and hawk dare never come;
They dare to fight like armies round their home.
The boughs will hardly bear their noisy guests
And storms will come and overturn the nests.
They build above the reach of clauming clowns:
They climb and feel but cunning cuts them down;
Others with reaching poles the nest destroys
While off and up they fly with deafening noise.

THE SEASONS

WRITTEN IN NOVEMBER

Autumn, I love thy latter end to view
In cold November's day so bleak and bare
When like life's dwindled thread worn nearly through,
Wi' lingering, pottering pace and head bleached bare,
Thou like an old man bids the world adieu.
I love thee well and often when a child
Have roamed the bare brown heath a flower to find
And in the moss clad vale and wood bank wild
Have cropped the little bell flowers palely blue
That trembling peeped the sheltering bush behind
When winnowing north winds cold and blealy blew.
How have I joyed wi' dithering hands to find
Each fading flower and still how sweet the blast
Would bleak November's hour restore the joy that's past.

SIGNS OF WINTER

'Tis Winter plain; the images around
Portentous[2] tell us of the closing year.
Short grows the stupid day, the moping fowl
Go roost at noon. Upon the mossy barn
The thatcher hangs and lays the frequent yaum,
Nudged close to stop the rain that drizzling falls
With scarce one interval of sunny sky
For weeks still leaking on that sulky gloom,
Muggy and close, a doubt twixt night and day.
The sparrow rarely chirps; the thresher pale
Twanks with sharp measured raps the weary frail,
Thump after thump, right tiresome to the ear.
The hedger lonesome brustles at his toil
And shepherds trudge the fields without a song.

The cat runs races with her tail, the dog
Leaps o'er the orchard hedge and knarls the grass;
The swine run round and grunt and play with straw,
Snatching out hasty mouthfuls from the stack.
Sudden upon the elm tree tops the crow
Unceremonious visit pays and croaks,
Then swops away. From mossy barn the owl
Bobs hasty out, wheels round and, scared as soon,
As hastily retires. The ducks grow wild
And from the muddy pond fly up and wheel
A circle round the village and soon tired
Plunge in the pond again. The maids in haste
Snatch from the orchard hedge the mizled clothes
And laughing hurry in to keep them dry.

---

[2] The MS has 'protentious'.

WINTER

The small wind whispers through the leafless hedge
Most sharp and chill while the light snowy flakes
Rests on each twig and spike of withered sedge
Resembling scattered feathers. Vainly breaks
The pale split sunbeam through the frowning cloud
On Winter's frowns below. From day to day
Unmelted still he spreads his hoary shroud
In dithering pride on the pale traveller's way,
Who croodling hastens from the storm behind
Fast gathering deep and black – again to find
His cottage fire and corner's sheltering bounds,
Where haply such uncomfortable days
Makes musical the wood-sap's fizzling sounds
And hoarse loud bellows puffing up the blaze.

THE WINTER'S COME

Sweet chestnuts brown, like soleing leather turn,
The larch trees, like the colour of the sun,
That paled sky in the Autumn seemed to burn.
What a strange scene before us now does run,
Red, brown, and yellow, russet, black, and dun,
White thorn, wild cherry, and the poplar bare,
The sycamore all withered in the sun.
No leaves are now upon the birch tree there,
All now is stripped to the cold wintry air.

See! not one tree but what has lost its leaves,
And yet the landscape wears a pleasing hue;
The Winter chill on his cold bed receives
Foliage which once hung o'er the waters blue;
Naked and bare, the leafless trees repose.
Blue headed titmouse now seeks maggots rare;
Sluggish, and dull, the leaf strewn river flows,
That is not green, which was so through the year;
Dark chill November draweth to a close.

'Tis Winter! and I love to read in-doors,
When the moon hangs her crescent upon high:
While on the window shutters the wind roars,
And storms like furies pass remorseless by.
How pleasant on a feather bed to lie,
Or sitting by the fire, in fancy soar,
With Milton, or with Dante to regions high,
Or read fresh volumes we've not seen before,
Or o'er old Burton's 'melancholy' pore.[3]

---

[3] Robert Burton's *Anatomy of Melancholy* (1621).

THE WINTER'S SPRING

The Winter comes, I walk alone;
I want no birds to sing.
To those who keep their hearts their own
The Winter is the Spring.
No flowers to please, no bees to hum;
The coming Spring's already come.

I never want the Christmas rose
To come before its time.
The seasons each as God bestows
Are simple and sublime.
I love to see the snow storm hing;
'Tis but the Winter garb of Spring.

I never want the grass to bloom;
The snow-storm's best in white.
I love to see the tempest come
And love its piercing light.
The dazzled eyes that love to cling
O'er snow white meadows sees the Spring.

I love the snow, the crimpling snow
That hangs on every thing;
It covers every thing below
Like white dove's brooding wing,
A landscape to the aching sight,
A vast expanse of dazzling light.

It is the foliage of the woods,
The dress that Winters bring –
White easter of the year in bud
That makes the Winter Spring;
The frost and snow his posies bring,
Nature's white spirits of the Spring.

THE WIND

The wind blows happily on every thing.
The very weeds that shake beside the fold
Bowing, they dance, do any thing but sing
And all the scene is lovely to behold:
Blue mists of morning, evenings of gold.
How beautiful the wind will play with Spring:
Flowers beam with every colour light beholds,
Showers o'er the landscape fly on wet pearl wings
And winds stir up unnumbered pleasant things.

I love the luscious green before the bloom,
The leaves and grass and even beds of moss,
When leaves 'gin bud and Spring prepares to come,
The ivy's evergreen, the brown green gorse,
Plots of green weeds that barest roads engross.
In fact I love the youth of each green thing:
The grass, the trees, the bushes and the moss
That pleases little birds and makes them sing.
I love the green before the blooms of Spring.

SPRING HAUNTS

I love to roam in Spring by hedgerow sides,
Those old enclosures mossed with many years
That wind by brooks and grassy close divides,
Where sheltered primrose earliest appears,
To mark the thorn unfold its crimpled green
And ash trees swell their yet black-buttoned buds
And I love paths that wind through tangling woods
Where bark ribbed maples, hazels all are seen
Mingling around their flushing hopes of leaves,
And where the ivy peers its blooms between
And round the oak its light-veined foliage weaves
There I would be as there I oft have been
To mark the things Spring's visits first employs
And breathe the raptures of her earliest joys.

MAY

Spring comes and it is May. White as are sheets
Each orchard shines beside its little town;
Childern at every bush a poesy meets,
Bluebells and primroses – wandering up and down
To hunt birds' nests and flowers a stone's throw from town
And hear the blackbird in the coppice sing.
Green spots appear like doubling a book down
To find the place again and strange birds sing
We have no name for in the burst of Spring.
The sparrow comes and chelps about the slates
And pops into her hole beneath the eaves
While the cock pigeon amorously awaits
The hen, on barn ridge cooing, and then leaves
With crop all ruffles – where the sower heaves
The hopper at his side his beans to sow;
There he with timid coveys harmless thieves
And whirls around the teams and then drops low –
While plops the sudden gun and great the overthrow.

SUMMER HAUNTS

I love in Summer time to seek a seat,
Wading the long grass where a path ne'er led,
Patting their downy tops with idle feet
And nodding blossoms, while around me fled
Insects, lone hermits of the peaceful grass,
Retreating further from approaching noise
Where large grasshoppers heavy bouncing pass,
Oft chased in idle sport of wanton boys;
And nimble beetles hasting everywhere,
From labour startled some and some from play;
Where butterfly darts up in gadding fear
And hoarse bee hummeth wearily away.
I love in Summer such lone haunts to seek
But feel regret their tenants' peace to break.

SUMMER AMUSEMENTS

I love to hide me on a spot that lies
In solitudes were footsteps find no track
To make intrusions – there to sympathize
With nature – often gazing on the rack
That veils the blueness of the Summer skies
In rich varieties—or o'er the grass
Behold the spangled crowds of butterflies
Flutter from flower to flower – and things that pass
In urgent travel by my still retreat,
The bustling beetle tribes – and up the stem
Of bents see lady cows with nimble feet
Climb tall church steeple heights or more to them
Till at its quaking top they take their seat
Which bows and off they fly fresh happiness to meet.

THE PLEASURES OF SUMMER

I love to drop in Summer on the grass
And with unwearied eye mark pleasing things:
To see the gadding swallow gaily pass,
Crumping the quiet lake with dipping wings
And list the restless cuckoo while it sings
In distant trees and nigh hand in the wood
That skirts its shadow o'er my mossy seat.
I love that pleasant rustling noise to meet
That tells of happiness with more than me:
Of fluttering linnets, this year's Summer brood,
That 'scaped the schoolboys' eye and fly to greet
Their happy parent hasting home with food,
As I do love such pleasing things to see
And in one's thoughts such pleasures to repeat.

A LARE AT NOON

I love it well in Summer hours
To trace the peaceful wood,
To shun the evils of the earth
And share of what is good;
To cast the bitter draught aside
Which care is daily giving
And seek the joys unstained wi' pride
Of nature and of heaven:

Where the poor squatting hare is blest
With what this life supplies,
Loved haunts that give her wanderings rest
Which cruel man denies;
Where nature's quiet luxury shoots
Her blossoms for the bee,
There too she mosses round the roots
A heavenly seat for me.

There with a book I love to be
And sit for hours together,
Or watching things that share wi' me
The Summer's lovely weather;
To see each humming nameless fly
Among the branches play
Or bright green beetles bustling by
On travel faraway;

And red and yellow lady cows,
I often do delight
To see them trot up weeds and boughs
To such a spacious height,
Or smooth bullrushes' taper stem
Till reached the very top

A steeple's height or more to them
Yet sees no fear to stop.

And on a mossy bank reclined
I often love to lie
To watch leaves twitter in the wind
And clouds pass in the sky
And green grasshoppers' vaulting springs
I've watched wi' wild surprise,
And counted colours in the wings
Of settling butterflies;

And hid me 'neath the crimpled brake
Where nightingales have sung
To watch the wary songster take
Its morsel to its young
And oft where blackthorn closely weaves
My leisure's been employed
To seek its dark eggs rapt in leaves
And left them undestroyed;

And where grass hides the leafy walks
And holds the dew for hours
Where kecks lift high on hollow stalks
Their multitude of flowers,
Where shadows round me as in play
To soft winds gently sweep
And peace beneath spread mosses grey
I've sat on stulps to sleep;

And on snug thickets' sward at ease
O'erhung wi' many a bough
Of hazel bush and oaken trees
I've lain me down as now

While swimming in my half-closed eye
The Summer's joys would seem
To pass and pass unceasing by
Like pictures in a dream,

Forms shadowing life still flitting by
At visioned fancy's will
And fast as moments breathe and die
Fresh forms creating still:
What taste oft sees in fancy's sleep,
Perhaps of fairy birth,
Things garmented in mysteries deep
That have no place on earth.

Who has not felt the joys I feel,
Left in this secret nook
Which willows from the path conceal
And thorns that hide the brook,
Stretched on the green grass free from noise
Save sounds of pleasant things,
Reading the pictured thoughts and joys
Which musing fancy brings.

Who has not felt that ecstasy
That fancy's power employs
In peopling Edens wild and free
As schoolboy hope enjoys –
Those scenes of mild eternity
With which her joys abound
Which dreams unveil of mystery
And smile in beauty round?

SUMMER BEAMING FORTH

I love to see the Summer beaming forth
And white wool rock clouds sailing to the north;
I love to see the wild flowers come again
And mare blobs stain with gold the meadow drain,
And water lilies whiten on the flood
Where reed clumps rustle like a wind-shook wood;
Where from her hiding place the moorhen pushes
And seeks her flag nest floating in bull rushes.
I like the willow leaning half way o'er
The clear deep lake to stand upon its shore.
I love the hay grass when the flower head swings
To Summer winds and insects' happy wings
That sport about the meadow the bright day
And see bright beetles in the clear lake play.

SUMMER

How sweet when weary dropping on a bank,
Turning a look around on things that be.
E'en feather-headed grasses spindling rank
A-trembling to the breeze one loves to see,
And yellow buttercups where many a bee
Comes buzzing to its head and bows it down
And the great dragonfly wi' gauzy wings
In gilded coat of purple, green or brown
That on broad leaves of hazel basking clings,
Fond of the sunny day – and other things
Past counting pleases one while thus I lie;
But still reflective pains are not forgot:
Summer sometime shall bless this spot when I
Hapt in the cold dark grave can heed it not.

SUMMER MORNING

I love to peep out on a Summer's morn
Just as the scouting rabbit seeks her shed
And the coy hare squats nestling in the corn,
Frit at the bowed ear tottering o'er her head;
And blundering pheasants that from covert spring,
Their short sleep broke by early trampling feet,
Making one sturtle wi' their rustling wings
As through the boughs they seek more safe retreat.
The little flower begemmed around wi' drops
That shine at sunrise like to burnished gold
So sweet to view the milk maid often stops
And wonders much such spangles to behold;
The hedger too admires 'em deck the thorn
And thinks he sees no beauties like the morn.

THE WHEAT RIPENING

What time the wheat field tinges rusty brown
And barley bleaches in its mellow grey
'Tis sweet some smooth mown baulk to wander down
Or cross the fields on foot path's narrow way
Just in the mealy light of waking day
As glittering dewdrops moist the maiden's gown
And sparkling bounces from her nimble feet,
Journeying to milking from the neighbouring town,
Making life light with song – and it is sweet
To mark the grazing herds and list the clown
Urge on his ploughing team with cheering calls
And merry shepherd's whistling toils begun
And hoarse-tongued bird boy whose unceasing calls
Join the lark's ditty to the rising sun.

MIST IN THE MEADOWS

The evening o'er the meadow seems to stoop;
More distant lessens the diminished spire;
Mist in the hollows reaks and curdles up
Like fallen clouds that spread – and things retire,
Less seen and less – the shepherd passes near
And, little distant, most grotesquely shades
As walking without legs – lost to his knees
As through the rawky creeping smoke he wades.
Now half way up the arches disappear
And small the bits of sky that glimmer through;
Then trees lose all but tops – I meet the fields
And now the indistinctness passes by.
The shepherd all his length is seen again
And further on the village meets the eye.

COLOURS OF AUTUMN

Now that the year is drawing to a close
Such mellow tints on trees and bushes lie
So like to sunshine that it brighter glows
As one looks more intently. On the sky
I turn astonished that no sun is there;
The ribboned strips of orange, blue and red
Streaks through the western sky a gorgeous bed,
Painting day's end most beautifully fair,
So mild, so quiet breathes the balmy air,
Scenting the perfume of decaying leaves
Such fragrance and such loveliness they wear –
Trees, hedgerows, bushes – that the heart receives
Joys for which language owneth words too few
To paint that glowing richness which I view.

VILLAGE LIFE

THE BUSY VILLAGE

The barn door is open and ready to winnow,
The woodman is resting and getting his dinner
And calls to the maiden with little to say
Who takes the hot dinner and hurries away;
The hens in the dust and the hogs in the dirt,
The mower is busy and stript in his shirt;
The waggon is empty and ready to start,
The ploughman is merry and drinking his quart;
The men are at work and the schoolboy at play;
The maids in the meadow a making the hay;
The ducks are a feeding and running about,
The hogs are a noising and try to get out;
The dog's at his bone and the ass at his tether
And cows in the pasture all feeding together.

THE VILLAGE IN SPRING

The cowboy sees the Spring and hears the crows
And cocks his hat and whistles as he goes;
The maidens hurry to the hedge and play
To catch the clothes the shower has blown away;
The horse leaps up, the cows no longer dull,
The maids bring home the buckets brimming full;
The old cow tosses up the gate away
And seeks the pasture where the Summer lay;
The ploughman often stops and wipes his brow
And sits and eats his luncheon on the plough;
The traveller birds in all directions fly
And winds no longer moan a desert sky;
The ploughman blundering on robust and strong
Makes faces at the wind and lobs along.

THE WOODMAN COMES HOME

The cake, turned oft till both sides brown, awaits
The supper hour as some are out till late
And night oft hears the pheasant's roosting crow
Ere woodmen that have even miles to go
Make their night faggots up; the cottage door
Opened and shut for twenty times & more
By expectation ere he comes – and all,
Soon as they hear the rustling faggot fall,
Up from the stools rush out – who first shall be
To meet their father's smile and know 'tis he.
The youngest first with many an eager stretch
Lifts up its arm in vain the latch to reach
While others laughing so the race to win
Bob up the latch as first to let him in.

THE HERD IS COME

The merry childern shout the herd is come
And run away to see the cows go home;
The village fills with all the lowing troop
And many a maiden with her gown tucked up
Stands ready at the gate to let them in
Where hodge is waiting with his dinner tin;
They make a lowing noise till night is o'er
And smell of pastures as they past the door;
Then maiden milks and then her song begins
And loud the new milk rattles in the tins;
They switch their tails and splash the maiden's face
And often get her cap in sad disgrace;
The herding boy with laughter on his brow
Will often ride upon the tamest cow.

THE SUMMER SHOWER

I love it well, o'ercanopied in leaves
Of crowding woods, to spend a quiet hour
And where the woodbine weaves
To list the Summer shower

Brought by the south west wind that balm and bland
Breaths luscious coolness loved and felt by all
While on the uplifted hand
The rain drops gently fall,

Now quickening on and on; the pattering woods
Receive the coming shower, birds trim their wings
And in a joyful mood
The little woodchat sings;

And blackbird squatting in her mortared nest
Safe hid in ivy and the pathless wood
Pruneth her sooty breast
And warms her downy brood;

And little pettichap like hurrying mouse
Keeps nimbling near my arbour round and round.
Aye; there's her oven house
Built nearly on the ground,

Of woodbents, withered straws and moss and leaves
And lined with downy feathers. Safety's joy
Dwells with the home she weaves,
Nor fears the pilfering boy.

The busy falling rain increases now
And sopping leaves their dripping moisture pour
And from each loaded bough
Fast falls the double shower.

Weed climbing hedges, banks and meeds unmown
Where rushy fringed brooklet easy curls
Look joyous while the rain
Strings their green suit with pearls

While from the crouching corn the weeding troop
Run hastily and huddling in a ring;
Where the old willows stoop
Their ancient ballads sing

And gabble over wonder's ceaseless tale,
Till from the south west sky showers thicker come,
Humming along the vale,
And bids them hasten home.

With laughing skip they stride the hasty brook
That mutters through the weeds until it gains
A clear and quiet nook
To greet the dimpling rain

And on they drabble all in mirth not mute
Leaving their footmarks on the elting soil
Where print of sprawling foot
Stirs up a tittering smile

On beauty's lips who, slipping mid the crowd,
Blushes to have her ankle seen so high,
Yet inly feeleth proud
That none a fault can spy;

Yet rudely followed by the meddling clown
Who passes vulgar gibes – the bashful maid
Lets go her folded gown
And pauses half afraid

To climb the stile before him till the dame,
To quarrel half provoked, assails the knave
And laughs him into shame
And makes him well behave.

Bird nesting boys o'ertaken in the rain
Beneath the ivied maple bustling run
And wait in anxious pain
Impatient for the sun

And sigh for home; yet at the pasture gate
The molehill-tossing bull with straining eye
Seemeth their steps to wait
Nor dare they pass him by,

Till wearied out high over hedge they scrawl
To shun the road and through the wet grass roam
Till wet and draggled all
They fear to venture home.

The plough team wet and dripping plashes home
And on the horse the ploughboy lolls along
Yet from the wet grounds come
The loud and merry song.

Now 'neath the leafy arch of dripping bough
That loaded trees form o'er the narrow lane
The horse released from plough
Naps the moist grass again.

Around their blanket camps the gypsies still
Heedless of showers while blackthorns shelter round
Jump o'er the pasture hills
In many an idle bound.

From dark green clumps among the dripping grain
The lark with sudden impulse starts and sings
And 'mid the smoking rain
Quivers her russet wings.

A joy-inspiring calmness all around
Breathes a refreshing sense of strengthening power
Like that which toil hath found
In Sunday's leisure hour

When spirits all relaxed, heart sick of toil,
Seeks out the pleasant woods and shadowy dells
And where the fountain boils
Lie listening distant bells.

Amid the yellow furze, the rabbits' bed,
Labour hath hid his tools and o'er the heath
Hies to the milking shed
That stands the oak beneath

And there he wiles the pleasant shower away
Filling his mind with store of happy things –
Rich crops of corn and hay
And all that plenty brings.

The cramped horizon now leans on the ground,
Quiet and cool, and labour's hard employ
Ceases while all around
Falls a refreshing joy.

HAY MAKING

'Tis hay time and the red complexioned sun
Was scarcely up ere blackbirds had begun
Along the meadow hedges here and there
To sing loud songs to the sweet smelling air,
Where breath of flowers and grass and happy cow
Fling o'er one's senses streams of fragrance now,
While in some pleasant nook the swain and maid
Lean o'er their rakes and loiter in the shade;
Or bend a minute o'er the bridge and throw
Crumbs in their leisure to the fish below.
Hark at that happy shout – and song between!
'Tis pleasure's birthday in her meadow scene.
What joy seems half so rich from pleasure won
As the loud laugh of maidens in the sun?

THE IDLE SHEPHERD BOY

The shepherd boy with little else to do
Makes heaps of dust and drags them in his shoe,
Then takes his knife and makes new places deep
And lays his stones and mortar on the heap
And thinks himself the greatest man alive
To build and play and study and contrive;
Then builds again and waits awhile when done
And leaves his labour drying in the sun;
Then makes his men of clay and bids them march
And drags the dust away and leaves an arch
And drags his cannon o'er with much renown
And loaded wagons till he breaks it down,
Then builds another up a finer way
And bids his sheep to wait and eat and play.

WINTER FIELDS

O for a pleasant book to cheat the sway
Of Winter – where rich mirth with hearty laugh
Listens and rubs his legs on corner seat,
For fields are mire and sludge and badly off
Are those who on their pudgy paths delay.
There striding shepherd seeking driest way,
Fearing night's wetshod feet and hacking cough
That keeps him waken till the peep of day,
Goes shouldering onward and with ready hook
Progs oft to ford the sloughs that nearly meet
Accross the lands. Croodling and thin to view
His loath dog follows; stops and quakes and looks
For better roads, till whistled to pursue,
Then on with frequent jump he hirkles through.

PLOUGHMAN SINGING

Here morning in the ploughman's songs is met
Ere yet one footstep shows in all the sky,
And twilight in the east, a doubt as yet,
Shows not her sleeve of grey to know her by.
Woke early, I arose and thought that first
In winter time of all the world was I.
The old owls might have hallooed if they durst,
But joy just then was up and whistled by
A merry tune which I had known full long,
But could not to my memory wake it back,
Until the ploughman changed it to the song.
O happiness, how simple is thy track.
–Tinged like the willow shoots, the east's young brow
Glows red and finds thee singing at the plough

WINTER EVENING

The crib stock fothered, horses suppered up
And cows in sheds all littered down in straw,
The threshers gone, the owls are left to whoop.
The ducks go waddling with distended craw
Through little hole made in the henroost door;
And geese with idle gabble never o'er
Bate careless hog until he tumbles down,
Insult provoking spite to noise the more;
While fowl high perched blink with contemptuous frown
On all the noise and bother heard below.
Over the stable ridge in crowds the crow,
With jackdaws intermixed known by their noise,
To the warm woods behind the village go
And whistling home for bed go weary boys.

BED TIME

The noisy blathering calves are fed and all
The cows are fothered up and in their stall.
Weary with toil and plodding through the mire,
The ploughman all are round the kitchen fire;
One pats the shaggy dog between his legs,
Another throws a crust to one that begs;
One sings a song and strokes in highest glee
The tabby cat that sits upon his knee;
One cracks about his horses and his plough;
One kisses Dolly 'cause he milked her cow;
Another has a smutty word to say
And makes the maiden blush and turn away,
Till every song is sung and tale is said;
Then maids lap up the fire and all to bed.

TO THE RURAL MUSE

Simple enchantress, wreathed in Summer blooms
Of slender bent stalks topped wi' feathery down,
Heath's creeping fetch and glaring yellow brooms
And ash keys wavering on thy rushy crown.
Simple enchantress, how I've wooed thy smiles,
How often sought thee far from flushed renown,
Sought thee unseen where fountain waters fell,
Touched thy wild reed unheard, in weary toils;
And though my heavy hand thy song defiles
'Tis hard to leave thee and to bid farewell.

Simple enchantress, ah, from all renown,
Far, far, my soul hath warmed in bliss to see
The varied figures on thy Summer gown
That nature's finger works so witchingly:
The silken leaf, the varied coloured flower,
Green nestling bower bush and high towering tree,
Brooks of the sunny green and shady dell.
Ah, sweet full many a time they've been to me
And though my weak song falters, sung to thee,
I cannot, wild enchantress, bid farewell.

Still feign to seek thee though I wind the brook
When morning sunbeams o'er the waters glide
And trace thy footsteps in the lonely nook
As evening moists the daisy by thy side.
Ah, if I woo thee on thy bed of thyme,
If courting thee be deemed ambition's pride,
Ah, 'tis so passing sweet wi' thee to dwell,
If love for thee in clowns be called a crime,
Forgive presumption – O thou queen of rhyme;
I've loved thee long; I cannot bid farewell.

GLOSSARY

baulk, strip of grass left unploughed

Bedlam cowslips, paigles (*Primula elatior*) though
   Robinson suggests false oxlip (*Primula x vulgaris*)

bent, grass stalk

black-nosed bee, probably the carpenter bee

blea, bleak, chilly

blow, blossom, as in 'in blow'

brustles, bustles about, makes a great fuss or stir

bumbarrels, long-tailed tits

checker, chequer

chelp, chirp

clauming, grasping, clutching

closen, enclosures

copple crown, tuft of feathers on the head of a bird

cot, cottage

crib stock, animals being fed from mangers

croodling, huddling together for warmth

crumping, knocking

elting, doughy, damp

fetch, vetch

fothered, foddered, fed

frail, flail

frit, frightened

furze, gorse

ground lark, probably the meadow pipit

hapt, wrapped, covered

hing, hang

hirkles, limps, moves with difficulty

kecks, umbellifers like cow-parsley and hogweed

knarl, nibble, bite at

lady cow, ladybird

lady-smock, cuckoo flower

lairs, places where the cows have lain

land, one of the strips into which a field was divided

lare, shelter, place to rest, bed

ling, heather

lob, walk heavily

mare blobs, marsh marigold

mizled, damp

oddling, the last of a set, the one left behind

nap, to nip, bite

peasecod, pea pod

peg morris, nine men's morris, a children's game played with pegs or stones on a shape scratched in the ground

pettichap, chiffchaff

pewet, lapwing

pilewort, lesser celandine

plat, plot

poesy, both posy of flowers and poetry

pooties, snail shells

prog, prod, poke

pudge, small puddle, ditch

rapt, wrapped, enclosed

rathe, early

rawky, misty, foggy, damp, raw and cold

reaks, smokes

scrawl, crawl, move with difficulty

shed, home territory, shade, shelter

soleing leather, leather to make the soles of shoes

sosh, plunge suddenly, dip in flight

starnel, starling

stuff, coarse woven fabric

stupid, deadened, dull

sturt, start, startle

sugh, a soughing or sighing noise

swaily, shady, cool

swath, the grass that falls at one sweep of the scythe

swee, sway

swop, swoop, fly

tenting, looking after

twanks, slaps smartly

water blob, marsh marigold

whitethorn, hawthorn

yaum, length of twisted straw used in thatching

INDEX OF FIRST LINES

Lightning Source UK Ltd.
Milton Keynes UK
UKOW05f1604251113

221781UK00001B/1/P